Selected Poems

Andrew Johnston

Selected Poems

ANDREW JOHNSTON

TE HERENGA WAKA
UNIVERSITY PRESS

Te Herenga Waka University Press
Victoria University of Wellington
PO Box 600 Wellington
teherengawakapress.co.nz

A catalogue record is available at the National Library
of New Zealand.

ISBN 9781776920693

Printed in Singapore by Markono Print Media Pte Ltd

Contents

from How to Talk (1993)

from The Sounds (1996)

from Birds of Europe (2000)

from Sol (2007)

from Fits and Starts (2016)

ECHO IN LIMBO

for Jenny Bornholdt and Greg O'Brien

FROM

How to Talk

1993

Revisionism

1. *The Present Tense*

The most important scenes are staged
on a particular stretch of coast.

While I am audience the hill is backdrop;
we change places often, however,

and soon the coast is
littered with costumes. That's the hat

where first we met, the shoes
that never fitted. And so on

and back again. We find many uses
for the rocks on the beach.

We refuse to make plans,
forget the script entirely.

2. *The Possessive*

Chance meetings provide
a series of places

to misunderstand each other.
In the car I am learning fast

how much I already knew
but there are gaps in the syllabus,

holes in the tent, and the wind
is cold and relentless.

Like turning up at the right time
and forgetting your own name: imagine.

3. *The Dark Past*

We both know why I
flinch as you press

a hand against my chest
and it isn't culture shock.

I'm left with
your attitude:

forehead tilted toward
the places where

the stars should be;
the whole of your serious profile

translated by the moon, reads
like an excess of strategy

and there, you say, I go again
and so I almost went,

slipping into the dark past
for the sake of comparison.

When I leave I leave
a lot to be desired.

4. *The Third Person*

After they had talked
there were five minutes left.

He watched them.
He felt the whole world

was coming to
the wrong conclusion

about him. Methodically.
Sleeping and waking:

one of those circles
night describes.

He couldn't
point to it

and smile
at the same time.

Visiting the House-To-Be

The house-to-be is more or less
or both. Its timbers frame
a little temple, it is skeletal,
smells of metal meeting wood.

Twos and threes adding up to eight
get out of an old green car,
most quite small. The site's pegged
mounds and trenches swarm.

Futures not exactly fitting but
sometimes touching, the eldest humming
on the violin where his room will be,
the second sizing up the yard, coming in

to bowl. Where are the others?
Our father fences off the quarter acre
in his mind, our mother has the blueprint,
checks the work. It measures up.

The Third Man

The moon men came down in time for the news.
Four. A woman's hands busy at the bench

of pumpkin, spud, out of sight of a boy,
five, small. Occasional drawl of a moon man

above the white noise, of suds sucked down
a plughole, space laughing in the black gap

below Apollo Eleven. The boy
told his teacher he'd be Michael Collins,

the third one, orbiting, silent. Twice, because
she wasn't sure she'd heard what he was saying.

Clair de Lune

He played the solitary lad
(he was always playing a part).
He played the solitary lad
but it was a large family,
he had to take himself off

on his bike or simply
find an empty room
and sit there for a while,
thinking of the stage. His
mind was full of corners.

He played Harold
and the arrow,
Maui and the hook,
he played This Old Man
and Peter Pan,

Clair de Lune and
Captain Cook—he
played them silently
so none of the family
would be disturbed. But

he was a bad actor. He stole
money for lollies and
hid in the dark thinking
This is the life, then
So this is the life.

Chip

Paul whose dad said
watch your language, don't
go getting any
big ideas.

1) A small piece removed.
2) The place where such a chip has been made.

Paul's dad, and Paul.
He let him know all about it.
He gave him a piece of his mind.

Pastorale

Into each life some rain must fall
but April was the wettest on record.

There's something to be said, they say,
for looking on the bright side

but the stock get carried away
by seasonal fluctuations,

the river wants to cover the field.
I've a good mind to get out

the dusty tuba father blew,
to play it by ear till the cows come home.

House and Garden

I can never remember
the names of the flowers

but Sylvia is in her
element here—the garden

after rain giving back
the house the shape it had.

Alonsoa, polyanthus . . .
each a bright coin

to spend in conversation.
The way they roll off the tongue.

New House

A subset of the whole, we gathered
in a corner of the architecture,
listening with a smile to the sound,
as heard inside the skull of the house,
of the train, or was it rain,
the sound of one enclosing the other

as much as we resembled each other
or Mother, or Father, we gathered
these thoughts unto ourselves. The rain
made an angle with the architecture
then followed the train. In the new house
the new maths, then history: a sound

sleep interrupted by nightmares, the sound
of sirens. One day broke off from another
as years began to fill the house
with sharp unspoken things, a decade gathered
speed, inventing its own peculiar architecture.
Tiny disappointments fell like rain.

So it began: tuneless engine of the rain
cranked by the wind. The culture came to sound
us out, believing a kind of spiritual architecture
could solve our problems with space, the other
side of the coin. Where two or three are gathered:
someone stood holding the door of God's house

while we delved in books for a porch to house
our doubts, a drought relieved by the physical rain
that fell inside our physical brains, and gathered

in pools in our limbs and glances. Did we sound
relieved, released into that other
garden, its blank leaves, its classical architecture?

Bob chose biology, Archibald architecture,
the body, the mind. A largely empty house
left behind to dream of other
journeys, Mother and Father and a rain
of reminiscence, an amber song. The sound
this made a soothing sound, we gathered.

As wind checked the architecture, a brother studied rain
falling on his own new house, and heard a familiar sound,
another family, as photographs and darkness gathered.

How to Talk

It was on the ferris wheel
I was introduced to

the art of conversation.
She was thirteen,

I was fourteen;
many times we passed the point where we'd climbed on.

How high it is, up here, she said
when we were near the top.

I could see my name
on the tip of my tongue.

Time Slides

Time slides
a muscle beneath the skin,

love smiles on the falling bodies.
They are falling in love, a sound

like the word voice,
sound of the air

filling the air.
A net of lies will catch them

and softly
let them through.

Walnut

I may as well make myself comfortable
with everything I know about you.

Here it is in a nutshell—
the nut having been eaten.

(One of us must have been
looking the other way.)

Was it a walnut?
Like a little brain.

One could never understand,
the other could never explain.

The Telephone

From you have I been absent in the spring
but there's always the telephone. Hello

what time is it there? There's an echo,
it's you, it's euphony, it's funny

how the way you say Here and
Hello and Hope, I can hear the H hatch

under your breath. How
do we navigate calmly the air

between us, the gaps between letters,
this turbulent alphabet.

The Reader, A Loved One

I waited in another place.
You were not there either.

I was your guest there.
The silence was like a silver tray.

In your absence I rehearsed both parts.
You would understand.

I wanted to make up for our lack of history.
All those dates we missed.

The river passed on its deep regrets.
But in other places resembled laughter.

November

1

Two spend aluminium time untouched,
a few fine days. The river mutters

this way. This way. High clouds boil
to feathers, flags, high west winds un-

weave them. Days in series,
personnel in parallel

meet and meet and never meet.
Twilight the blue leaves, then darkness:

November the moon shone in German,
a mushroom light illicit and harmless.

2

A woman, a plain man
laughing, adrift—

a raft of thirty days,
November's

ash afloat on a
disused dam,

a wren in
the brain, a gull

beneath the
tongue.

3

Flax flowers for
a certain bird,

headfeathers
yellow with pollen—

as if it didn't
come to drink.

Warm winds flatten the grass,
the house aches alongside:

it is an idea,
all month they think it over.

4

He climbed aboard the brown train
because it was about to depart.

He climbed down
from the brown train

because it was
about to depart.

Dogs barked, and bells rang
and soon the train was gone.

The band struck up another
twentieth century classic.

The Seminar on Originality

Just to make them smile, now, rather than agree
we trawl in the lake's layers of coldness, inattentive,
for well-preserved points of view, decked out
with sensory apparatus, in working order, for them to play on
while we get on with the cold wet work that is its own
        reward.

It's not as if our hopes had been scuttled, after all
the water rose around them where they'd settled
somewhere between question time and geological time
as pearls form, or gallstones, and they were wishes
inadvertently come true, more so than we would have hoped.

And if the instructions are brought up intact, but don't tally
with the versions handed down, has a need been identified
to revise our expectations, our method of proceeding
on the basis of conflicting evidence, wearing several hats
and sporting several badges? The answer's coming up

in the next bucket, which is always the one after this one.
Meanwhile a small boy is coming to the door. At the end
of the seminar on originality, the young Freudian
—you should have been there—turned and said 'Well
what about the atomisation of the individual?' At the time
I felt completely atomised, but now I know exactly what he
        meant.

The Poetry Inspector

has been sent by the tradition
to check our nails. His are impeccable

as his crisp tones, which come to a point
somewhere over the horizon. This

is called verse perspective
says the verse detective

filing his ironies.
He says we're menaced by

nebulosities
and smiles;

he can tell us if our poems have class,
whether our nails fail or pass.

We should render our caesuras
to the things that are England's

encapsulates the tenor of his findings;
he sometimes spares a word of praise

for good measure—
it should be said

the poetry inspector
sometimes hits the nail on the head.

Haiku Beach

a place to stop for
fuel, or for good, the people
very retiring

from here to the sea
slow down in the street, in the
supermarket aisle

along the beach road
River Glade, Park Avenue
Oak Bay, Walnut Close

fences and glimpses
architectural finish
magazine gardens

gap for the golf course
Toledo Park Motel, keep
your options open

five have formed a group
to walk the sand, a south wind
the cold light of day

recall the village
a book that caught your eye back
there, Ten Late Breakfasts

Fool Heart

1. *The evergreens*

Rich scents, guess—yes, the evergreens,
there is something in the wind,

it is blowing from the Dwarf Conifer Collection,
whistling *I wish*

IwishIwish
and never completes the sentence . . .

Shapes, shades, the Garden of Remembrance,
something out of stone—a hard look

at your fool heart, printed
with warnings.

2. *Sensible shoes*

Gravel, an avenue, a gate thrown open—
we've been down this path before.

Here you are, and
here: note this footprint's

toehold on the real, the whole
an accurate absence: it's yours

and so are these, where you went
in your sensible shoes, each neat outline

getting you ready
for the next step.

3. *The shallows*

A shag shakes, dives—for its other name
and comes up with *cormorant*, a bottle

rolls in the shallows—it's empty
for a moment—it's clear

you can't stay serious here.
The bay breaks into laughter, its surface

nervous as Mercury—god of scholars,
travellers, thieves,

is he after
your heart, the fool.

4. *True north*

North, true north, magnetic north—
don't ask the heart for directions,

lost in the forest. New leaves
put themselves out for you,

for your trouble, for your
fool heart, filling itself

with meaning.
Tell it to stay

an obedient tree
whose roots yet crack the path.

5. *Stern bird*

Stern bird sings—at the top of its twig
'I've come to see the done thing done'

Stern bird in the undergrowth,
listening . . .

A man goes by with a noisy heart—
I wish IwishIwish—

he might need a new frame of mind,
something to fit the facts:

stern bird in its tree,
fool heart in its cage of ribs.

6. *New view*

Sea like a lake today,
strait like a door, water

leaving of its own accord.
Here's a new view,

a hill of shale for a lover to look over,
a slope, a slight rise, a house over-

looking the harbour, its
points of departure, a port.

Here's a boatload of hope held up by customs,
a courtship caught before the boat could sail.

7. *Old magnolias*

A mind made free in the Main Garden goes
slowly over the sense of what you've said.

Old magnolias burst into Latin—
white flowers flare, fall silent, leaves all

point to their divinity, a pink tree
thinks nothing of such perfection. The eye

leads naturally to where the sky is clearing
above the Sundial of Human Involvement

which can be located next
to the Observatory.

The Sounds

1996

Visitors

A child is playing
at the edge of memory—in sand
behind a house
the child has made a river,
a trickle small
as the birth of the real

river, whose real
music the child hears playing
beyond the small
back yard—it tastes like sand,
the sound of the river,
and sounds like grown-ups talking in the house

with visitors. The house
seems huge, unreal
or holy, the river
made of metal and light, playing
from gold to sad silver, the sand
a trickle small,

a somehow to be trusted small
belief: it will outlast the house.
The child balanced in sand
at the edge of the real
hears visitors' voices, a strange record playing,
and sees a brother in the river

carrying a brother across the river—
how, from here, they both seem small.
Are they playing

a game, or should those in the house
be told, is this real
or something like sand

flowing through sand?
Halfway across the river
the brothers change places, a real
laugh, and then where are they? A small
bird flies from empty river to silent house,
the child goes back to playing

in tangible sand, in memory, a small
corner given over to the talkative river, the visited house
that for a while was real, the funny music the record was
       playing.

The Headline Writer
(Frank Johnston, 1901–1956)

Pages turning, over the sea:
the newspaper room where my grandfather sits

reading the *Listener* and hearing the reader
over the road in the Newspaper Room

whose eye is caught by a headline and
must turn back to finish the story

as if he went back in the night
to shut a banging gate

and found his grandfather
standing there.

Sonata

for Jenny Bornholdt and Greg O'Brien

In a dream it is very hard to read.
Things you'd never dream of
insist on showing themselves—
a tree that flies,
crouching in the garden;
the dragon-horse, likewise, doesn't help you

concentrate. Even the book, as you
force your eyes back to it, starts to read
itself badly—now it is a water garden,
now a bird with words for feathers. Lines of
print lift into flight—you wake, the book flies
off. How swiftly dreams erase themselves.

*

Gently days arrange themselves
around the views you have of them. Or you
forget to look, and time flies
anyway, or flows—a diary, to read
with a lifting heart, its pages of
notes—loose leaves—its private garden

turning, in visible wind, to a garden
of signs, of questions you ask yourselves
in the plural from now on, and discover new ways of
answering—the true and the kind—you
find everything doubled like this, you read
each word as if for the first time. And time flies.

*

On the windowsill it is always summer. Flies
forget what they were doing, garden
lemons ripen and sweeten. Postcards read
their postmarks in the glass, glimpse themselves
slipping through time zones. You
lean to scan the recipe there, meet the clean scent of

watercress, capsicum, musk of
olives, and a door in your mind flies
open, as memories find you
half in the kitchen, half in the garden
listening: home is the music you lose yourselves
in, a tune you both hear as you read,

*

of an evening, the same book. The wind in the garden
quietens, a moth flies into the light. And over the page—you
find yourselves smiling—and over the lines that, in a
        dream, were very hard to read.

For Rose

(*Rosie Marsland, b 26/7/94*)

What does sunlight sound like?
A white flower in darkness knows,

an ear that hears both ways, and sees—
sirens, and silence; laughter, and after;

conversation of insects all over the house
and a steady heart

thinking *the the the*
and Rose's ear, born furled, unfolds

that hears these, and those, and knows—
Rose listens to the world, the world listens to Rose.

Heaven
for Joseph Cornell

So many thought only of heaven,
sent their hopes there,
what they knew of the infinite,
heaven collapsed.

'Charts of the stars,
pipes, corks, thimbles,
indigo blue and milky white'—
no one knows they're bits of heaven,

no one's been there. So they end up
in some supporting role—
as houses near the Acropolis
incorporate old marble—

or some old prayer recycles itself
right into your life: you're walking along
and a perfect stranger suddenly smiles—
hell, it's so embarrassing,

and it feels like heaven, and it is.

Boat

A boat though no more than a thought
might carry us, far from

the coast, as far as
we know. But

is it a ship then,
cresting and sounding? I think,

for its boasting, it's just a boat
drifting down a difficult river—

now and then it runs aground
and that is where we live.

Gourd

How much could such a word hold—
for storage, or music—

a word like *gourd*,
a thought seen only when it slows

like light through a lens, or liquid
changing the sound of its

hollow container, as speech
when words are in this mood

suddenly cups
something startling.

Tired and Emotional

Darkness kept you up at night
then daylight wouldn't let you sleep,
shining its sun in your eyes. Yet
weariness like this might lay down such paths
as lead to the discovery of a whole
new music. It's been waiting for all

your chatty certainties to shut up, all
those smooth fingers of manner and night,
the white and the black keys, the whole
rehearsal's endless orchestra to sleep,
so that a single note, where these paths
intersect, might usefully reverberate yet

within us—can you hear it?—and yet
without us. You have to listen with all
your life. Stick to the footpaths
for the rest of the day, and the following night
it becomes a simple lullaby; you sleep
reminded of how you might be whole

despite the evidence, and your whole
body will thank you. Yet
some things a good night's sleep,
you find, is bad for, after all:
that tune that was there all night
in your dreams has gone, down which paths

you'll never know, except that they were the paths
of forgetfulness, and it was the whole
number corresponding, in the depths of night,

to the sound you'd heard when you weren't ready yet,
tired and emotional, the day before, all
washed up and longing for sleep,

the sound of your self. And if sleep
hasn't sent it packing, down those paths
we spoke of, it will be drowned now by all
the new day's noises, as the part meets the whole
theme's needs then dies. And won't be back. Yet
perhaps, such days suggest, if you stay up all night

now and then, and sleep later, the whole
maze of paths that connect your heart to the world might
        yet
begin to reveal all, in the slow room of a day that follows a
        sleepless night.

Knowledge

A damp fact, earthen, papery.
He closed his mouth when he had finished speaking.

One thought of all the deaths in that instant,
another the shouts and collisions,

everything seen from so far it seems soundless:
a runner reaching the ribbon—

it winds itself around him,
momentum overwhelming the moment

as when, sometimes, the lights having failed,
traffic flows more freely.

Prime Time

1.

Evening clouds like schools of thought;
great philosophers put to good use
changing the light bulbs up there—
clear, or pearl? They always choose pearl.

2.

'The grey clouds and the pink
elope through dusk to marry in the dark'—
the clematis, for this sentence,
awards itself white stars.

The Sounds

Rain, a restful place: a plain
negotiation led to this, one small
lit room, in lieu of a camera, and the
drowned valleys, windless, listening
to the rain, on leaf, on water
in winter. Disentangled thus, we touch

as if deciphering a prophecy, we touch
as ocean, held by the land, made plain
a difficult map, whose cove-smooth water
uncoils with travel, surrounds a small
arrival, a larger departure. Listening
to the sounds as we pronounce them, the

waves, the bright particulars, we hear the
way we've been so far, we touch
speech, our bodies fearless listening
devices. And days unravel as on a plain
a road will travel straight with small
perceptible corrections. But water

under the hand of the wind, and water
in darkness: things we see and cannot tell, the
sounds are full of these too, as small
fish, late, in a bell of light, touch
the surface once and disappear. It's plain
each morning, talking and not listening

how plain things aren't, how whether we're listening
or not, the sounds go on around us, and water
will erase all previous arrangements. It's plain

how prophecies succumb before the
evidence, words in sand that crumble at a touch,
that need to be unwritten or forgotten, and small

reliable ambitions fashioned, parts for a small
cast—two, who move from stage to stage, listening
to the places where their different futures touch.
Rain-fast, a stream falls, to clear salt water
where just such a lean crew rows, the
dinghy iffing and butting, a plain

afternoon. The small boat drums the mingling water;
the rowers, listening, will remember the
sounds, when they touch, that these days made plain.

You Will Be Able to Sleep Here

Such subtle interruptions—
three trees (their lack of speech

an incomplete complaint),
a bird left to writing—

some of her sayings thus
beautifully unfinished, each

utterance plucked by the wind
as though—not a god, Diana—

she took another arrow from her quiver
while the first was still in the air.

Clomp

It was hard to sleep at the edge of the forest.
What did you think you were hearing,

head against her chest—a woman in
loose boots wading through paper—

clomp, rustle—her heart?—
the night was full of it,

then Dawn came through the door, or
didn't, which is why you woke—

the neighbour's irrigation pump, the
tent, still dark, whispering something . . .

In White

She came so close—so curious—
he thought he'd caught the scent of her thinking.

She said her heart, a bird—in white—
had long since left the nest, because it was restless

and hadn't returned
so he built a screen in white

around her heartlessness:
these are the hopeless movies he projected

because she offered nothing
and he accepted.

Caretaker

You grasp what a child is saying,
then you're in the pool—

running in a circle
to stir the chemicals in;

a current comes around behind, so cold
(you're learning to swim).

A man stands at the edge who
tipped the sky-coloured crystals in,

who took care of memory—
memory takes care of him.

Flora

From mind to pond,
our doubt, our flora—

our mute invisible daughter
stood over the water

lost in reflection, but
the sun shone

in our eyes and she was gone.
What did she see

deep, a glitter, the flash
of an idea?

A little stitch
looks for system—

I go over and over it
and am undone.

Try

Messages arrive every second.
The newspaper unfolds
like a bird, releasing
this picture: man on a swing,
the word TRY, his centre
of gravity, his smile. To try

sometimes you have to lean back: try
it. It's hardly second
nature, but already you've left the centre:
the story you told yourself unfolds
around you, and the swing
brings you back again and again, releasing

memories like a tree releasing
seeds. You watch a bird, in stillness, try
to crack one open, the swing
of its beak against stone, the second
hand ticking as morning unfolds,
the slight cavity you imagine at the centre

of each seed like the silence at the centre
of each word, the gas language releasing
inaudible atoms whose motion unfolds
only in your sleep. To try
is to try to understand, every second,
and then you're on the swing,

leaning back. You think you'll learn to swing
your body gently through the house, from one centre
of attention to the next; your second

wind will come along in time, releasing
the necessary parachute—you'll try
to read what's written there as it unfolds—

and the long descent begins, the land unfolds
beneath you, somewhere a tree with a childhood swing
you're slowly floating back to . . . Don't try
to hold on to such a story. At its centre
a gap too wide to leap is releasing
another story, the second

a third, and so on, as the comedy unfolds,
reclaiming and releasing you to swing
until you're balancing: your centre of gravity, your smile,
      the word TRY.

Air

You dream in one country,
wake up in another.

Until you come to occupy
a kind of cloud, above the sea—

just you and your bicycle.
But its back tyre's a little flat.

Pump it up at the gas station,
someone suggests, but you give it

too much air: BANG, it splits
and something happens to your dreams, too—

one of them in a bike repair shop
and when you come out it's raining.

Fauna

After weeks of sun and wind and no rain,
everything loses its shape in the grass—

birds, shadows of birds, lovers, footballs.
As you watch, two deer run right up to the road

and freeze, gazing at traffic, almost disappearing.
Clouds roll up, the credits of a film you've just

slept through, so nothing makes sense
except these deer—so thin, so silent.

They turn and flee, like thought, back to the trees.
And then, as in the stories, it softly begins to rain.

Binoculars
for Marc Nielson

I was a stranger. But you look
familiar, people would say.

Big cars, big country. You need
binoculars, here, said a man, I can sell you some.

I took them back to my room
and watched hawks over the river,

sun reddening their tail feathers,
then I looked at everything in my room

through them, the wrong way round—
tiny photographs, books, tiny lamp—

which made me feel instantly philosophical,
distant, a little taller. Infinitely stranger.

Border
for Yuriy Stroykov

'With you I enter a distant land,'
the young man writes in his notebook,

'but much later, without you, I am lost.'
He stares out to sea, where the border floats,

courtesy of joint-venture fishing boats—
vodka bottles from Vladivostok,

local orange plastic buoys and bindings.
After a storm bits of border will litter the coast.

He'll never get across the sea, he thinks,
'I will send words instead'—

scowling and hissing at each other to keep up
lest they sink beneath the map.

Chord

A plucked string disappears
like a name said over and over,

a point on the soft arc of the surface
slipping down the river—a placename

marked by what flies over it. Distantly
pelicans circle—white, then gone

on account of the darkness under their wings
returning to strike a white chord: in agreement

everything coming together and suddenly
going through the same change.

Fall

Trail and trial had always given trouble.
Take the trail through autumn—

it led to the cemetery, and then a dog
came down the same trail,

startling the deer that grazed there. But
to see a deer leap headstones! Cheating

death like that, and the dog.
You wander around for a while—this is

the trial—trying to find a way out
for what seems like an eternity

until an angel covers his eyes and points.
By then it is winter;

you squint up at street signs,
which is like learning to read.

The Beginning of Winter

1. *White letters*

Daylight was broader there, maps
took a long time to unfold. When it snowed

thoughts took shape in
the spaces between

things we had a name for, as if
white letters had fallen, a language

only our anxious bodies heard, out
walking, arrangements of bones

that red flesh shivered to cover: the red,
the white, the cold, the broad daylight.

2. *Gravity*

Gravity lets us
take life lightly,

all night it made
clouds fall, dusted

the field with
frozen light, as if

someone had been
unpacking the moon

and all the
soft stuff that

stopped it rocking
was being

handed down
to us.

3. *Colours*

Light splinters in the cold, colours
slip into hiding. Red is in the animals,

a song they sing
over and over to stay warm. And green

sleeps in blue light under the snow
where a deer comes to scratch with its hoof

but won't survive.
Under the ice,

in our vague idea of the river
fish swim up and down in their constant knowledge.

4. *Drift*

The wind writes a paragraph about white,
snow coming down to cover both hands,

becoming the numberless page: on each leaf
a leaf of white,

a layer of belief. Days
crystallise, dissolve—

you walk out to the end of each
and stare into the dark drift. Eventually

a calm voice comes to you—
it is your voice.

Apple

To recollect, a green leap—
an apple in your hands. I try

to wrap time back around it, that
came off in one continuous strip

but it's gone, with a chuckle
like that of a shutter—there

must be a snap in existence, or
a likeness, on the street, who

grins at an apple and bites,
and finds the apple smiles back.

Coyote

How it howls on the plains,
creeps through the mountains—

I think coyote's
soul went into the car

the moment I killed it, white
water in darkness, running

into the flash. I pulled over
and howled; I think coyote's

soul went into me—as I wept
it climbed into the back seat

and whispered 'White man,
you kill me and I live.'

How to Walk

It's too late to tell you. Something
was missing, a long time ago,

and you had to work out a way of getting there—
one foot in front of the other, perhaps—

only to find more mysterious clues—
a coin, a hairclip, the Queen of Hearts—

suggesting another puzzle, in other words,
some of the pieces already lost. Walking's

like that: if you start to think about it
pretty soon you have to sit down.

Wire

Wire from here to the place you are from—
there, you can hear the wind in it,
humming. Saying 'from'
where the wire passes: grass, a road,

hubcaps in which
everything tips and disappears and returns.
A child in bright colours was walking there.
She is in some of the photographs,

looking up at the wire, the word on her tongue
sounding like a question
that knows it has no answer, the wire just a wire
going on and on.

FROM

Birds of Europe

2000

Fireflies

Sky white as the gap between chapters—
we were in lilac time,

just after dandelions,
light on the lake fume-blue.

Then we were in
the time of a flower

neither knew the name of. We lay
side by side, like drawn-up boats

on spring grass, warmed by assumptions
and a wind from the south-west.

*

If I could choose a beginning
how about the first ending,

the one that made
everything possible:

fireflies thick above the dark ditch,
switching on and off their

soft blue sparks:
were they courting

or merely
trying to avoid collisions?

Leaving

Taupata scrapes the house all night,
a madman brushing off spiders. You try

to fold the map small enough
to find a place to live, but

the wind prevails, fraying the sky,
making it hard to

read the directions. Outside
the day is ceramic, brittle—

a bright hood: its
crumbs of light.

*

Your belongings—
as if you belonged to them—

vanish as the funnel narrows:
you want to weigh down

a few precious things,
open the doors,

let the wind take the rest.
Days of boxes, allegorical days:

the sky turns its huge puzzled face towards you,
and then it turns away.

How to Fly

Try anything, like the young birds
—it's late spring—in the rose garden

falling and—just in time—recalling
something they haven't had time to learn

and carrying on this conversation
consisting of the word 'Yes.' Their

mothers lift beetles from the blooms' silk nests,
clean the buds of aphids; the young

fall and flap and open their pink silk mouths for food
and say 'Yes.' And then they fly.

London Winter

How the rain
shines on stone,

bare trees let the light through.
Each day's an attic, grey—

you bump your head on cloud.
The sun fades from star to rumour,

a red ball lost in fog.
Kneel and pray to the fire instead:

your wishes will be granted, as wishes are,
little by little.

Antipodean

Crocus buds come up out of winter,
whiteyellowpurple. Then night arrives,

black as a cab, its putter and gleam.
'Courage,' say the pub windows: inside

by the fire, old friends ask 'have I changed?'—
who want to hear Yes, who want to hear No.

The way we say Home, meaning here or there,
it's a well-lit word, it's open all hours,

but when we go home and turn out the light
we dream of crocuses opening.

The Moon at Kew

Wooden, conditional, over the Palm House—
what is it, with its spidery eye—

a catalyst, a listening post, a kite?
Who am I talking to? Who

is trying to turn the page I am writing on?
I fancy I can hear you breathing,

I fancy I can hear you shift in your chair.
O salt-lick. Clockface. Tide-mind.

To whom am I talking? I'll never know
you. I know you. Stay. Let's

call it by all its names
till it turns away:

Bitter pill. Eardrum. Fossil
that glows in the dark. Old stone flower.

The Singer

In the photograph on the back cover
of the singer's first album for seven years
he looks out through a rain-streaked window—
one half of his face,
blurred, smiles; the other,
troubled, is clear. He's turning away

slightly, as if to turn away
from himself. If you cover
one side of a photograph, then the other,
you sometimes see two people, years
of differences between them, the face
like hills at dawn from the window

of a plane. The singer leans on the window-
sill, awkward, staring. You look away,
recognising in the expression on his face
how imperfectly you can ever cover
the actual with the imagined self, despite years
of acting naturally: slips of the tongue, other

turns of phrase, add up to another
story. Through the shop window
an unfamiliar city lights up. For years
you stayed; how many went away
before you began to discover
you needed the same? And had to face

admitting that one side of your face
was deep in debt to the other,
that cantilevered promises could never cover

the distance from harbour window
to the view itself, a world away.
The singer's gaze surprises: the years

you loved his songs for their innocence were the years
you believed in your own; now his face
says: Everything can be taken away.
One bright eye resembles the shaded other
but neither is the window
of the soul; the glance is finally opaque, a cover-

ing. And the soul? Watch the face of another
watching you, for years; there's a chance you'll discover,
—singly, or together—a way to open the window.

Martinborough

for Peter Black and Mary Macpherson

A town planned on the Union Jack,
streets named after Mr Martin's
grand tour, 1879—
Panama, Texas, New York—gives way to

harp after harp of wires and vines. At
Walkers', a dachshund keeps the birds off,
nibbles the lowest grapes as they ripen:
a cutting they thought Syrah grew into

something entirely Unknown. They name
the wine Justa Red or Notre Vigne,
startlers that leap the fence and gallop
into the drinkable blue-black night—

the rest of the flag. Not many cars.
A few farms, like stars, to steer by.

About

You're right, it's time I said what it's about
Or rather said what I was about to say
Before these things got in the way
To which it was and is connected—
Let's unplug them one by one
Until a single small red light
Tells us that we've got it right—
The Subject's what it's all about.
But what if all the lights go out?
Which connection mattered most?
Or was it about nothing, really—
A poem's about a thing, ideally.
(This one—for the sake of simplicity—
Let's say it's about electricity.)

Cold

For three years it was winter.
I saw my brother there,

his face glazed with ice
through which his eyes

still tried to shine. He was
so cold he didn't know

it was winter for three years;
when his mind began to thaw

how his face
ran with tears.

The Singer

didn't sing, it whirred
and the smaller Singer—

like a child of the bird—
with which we stitched little

books, and stared . . .
Wondering—it isn't hard:

you ask yourself, you're
overheard, and over-

head a single word
that made you start

still makes you start,
as if someone broke a stitch

and in another room
the Singer stirred.

History

She was surrounded by objects at the time
and we all said too many words

but the boundaries of the occasion were thus
suitably padded, and

no one could remember, years later,
what anyone said or did, especially. Time passed

and went into a kind of depot
filled with mistakes not yet paid for;

trains went past in the night like dreams,
and then you were in one of them, driving.

At Angey

Mamie, Mémère
wade through the house—the years

come up to their waists, some days
the years come up to their shoulders

floating photographs from the mantel—
dead and living lit by the same light—

and when the years are thickest,
you imagine Mamie, Mémère—

as woodsmoke spreads like milk in the morning air—
push off and gently swim from room to room

because you know it's not like that—time
wrecks their knees and bends their backs, and

when the years rise high enough to carry them,
the years will carry them away.

Lapwing

I was like the lapwing—
a strange bird, from

'leap' and 'wink'—
crested in stubble, or

black in flocks rising. How
do I know? You

bought the guide
by which I might identify.

Winter I stay, they
just up and fly. But

look in the book—
a leap, a wink—

there they are. They
look me in the eye.

Sanctuary

for Gaby Gaidot 1991–1999

At the sanctuary, by the estuary
having crossed the coast, birds change their names.
Salt on its tongue, the river goes on drinking.

Spoonbill, plover, godwit—migratory—
flock and gossip, bathe and wade
at the sanctuary, by the estuary,

landing like a shower of arrows,
rising like blown foam.
Salt on its tongue, the river goes on drinking.

Rushes in green-brown waves as if painted
each with the tip of a rush
at the sanctuary, by the estuary;

anchored mid-channel, boats ride and ride
as if trying to decide.
Salt on its tongue, the river goes on drinking.

Birds ready feathers for flight, for new words.
One of us will never return
to the sanctuary, by the estuary.

I want to be still as the pond after wind,
I want to be still as the heron.
By the sanctuary, at the estuary,
salt on its tongue, the river goes on drinking.

Saudade

Saudade,
'the freedom to be sad'—

the very idea can make you glad,
and *lusophone*—hello?—

this is Portuguese speaking.
Ladies and gentlemen,

life is hard. But
there are grilled sardines for lunch—

we crunch their
delicate skeletons.

FROM

Sol

2007

Bonjour La France

for Peter Black
(Giverny 5/5/1998–Paris 22/12/2002)

As willows weep and lilies pose,
I see the artist's landscape decompose,

I see standers and waiters escape their fate,
I see a whole continent looking away,

I see the light betray Jesus
and Cool Water Woman,

and because the lens reflects
your fine grey sense

I see the hand of circumstance
everywhere. Bonjour la France.

Hypermarket

The carparks divide
into continents;
the staff skate around, inside,
with hyperconfidence.

You go in looking
for a clock or a pear
and emerge, hours later,
with a deck chair;

crossing the world
in search of the car
a fresh wind fills the canvas
somewhere off the coast of Africa.

Roundabout

Roundabouts, swings,
it was all one piece of luck to us—

yon hollow, crusted roundabout
with copper where the clamp was,

this great roundabout,
the world, with all its motley rout,

the brand-new roundabout at Ballygawley,
the first in mid-Ulster.

Stars all around suns turn roundabout.
Bright midges dance on wall.

*

An owl flew so low
in the valley of the Vire

our headlights lit its
wide white wings—

we gave way, and carried on,
roundabout after roundabout,

approaching each as
one approaches

a question or decision
and goes round it.

*

Once in fog on a long straight road
we came to such a junction,

the island a high mound covered in shrubs
and among them a sports car, driver beside it—

his look of stupefaction you'd know if
ever you'd blundered through speed and fog

right into the centre of the question
where it was dark and you were alone

with only the sound of engines,
the beating of wings.

*

In a letter addressed to
the Polish Friends of Animals

on the occasion of the erection
on Sunday, May 27, of a monument

in the likeness of Dzok, a dog
who waited nine months for his master

on a roundabout in Krakow,
Brigitte Bardot emphasises

'the extraordinary loyalty
of which only animals are capable'.

*

Little by little, it will be written,
Roundabout Man replaced Crossroads Man

on the uninhabitable planet
we now know as Roundabout

as the love of certainties
gave way to approximation

and the names he gave to his ignorance
adapted to the circumstance

living, as he did, half in darkness, half in light,
along the edge of knowledge.

*

The lift doors opened,
a woman stepped out:

he gave her his heart,
she gave it right

back, saying Here,
you might need this

and having gone
around the question,

met him on
the other side.

*

The astounding number of roundabouts
can make Canberra a dizzying experience.

In some of the very new suburbs,
even minor suburban streets

have their own
baby roundabouts.

The very word 'roundabout' can reduce
even a brave driver to tears after

a day's drive
in 'The Bush Capital'.

*

If you're not sure,
and who is, if

none of the signs,
and when do they,

carry on round, enjoy
the view, the

changing light, talk
among yourselves, eat

for example, an apple (the core,
miles later, still in your hand).

*

Entry flare and splitter island
distinguish the modern roundabout.

The future success of roundabouts
will depend on the roundabouts themselves.

There are about 40 roundabouts all over Utah.
I've heard rumours about a roundabout somewhere near
        Moab.

Professor Ragnvald Sagen explains the Norwegian
        experience
with roundabouts in winter. Price: $15.

Studies have determined that the safest way to proceed
        through a roundabout
is to walk your bicycle.

*

One day you'll get around to saying.
Then it will be time to leave

this place, or lack of a place,
with its unobstructed view

of beautiful obstructions,
of a limited number of options.

The barn owl or fright owl, a white owl,
nests in barns, lofts, ruins, belfries.

No one is coming. You cross the road
and step on to the dark grass circle.

Arch

A succession of doors in the air,
of raised eyebrows:

at Porte St-Martin and Porte St-Denis
Paris stops for the king, then goes on

walking in the country. Louis
who can't get away from his wedding—

those macaroons, those Spaniards. Why
did they brick up the door of the church?

The Sun King is fretting about the succession;
the Infanta just extends her arm—

oh, she says archly, surely
someone will come along.

Sol

Solitude, solace, consolation—
sun in its onlyness

shines on us here,
cups the heart in a deep blue bowl.

Courtyard radio. Swallows in pairs.
You'll have to let everything go

but it stays, and stays,
and is connected:

straight white line—no wind—a plane
flying, in the mind, towards the sun.

The Cyclist

Here she comes, or here he comes—
her enormous head wobbling towards us,
his fat little legs pumping the pedals . . .

They say her skin is whitening,
that she is losing her downy hair—
every day he grows younger:

soon he will be nothing,
soon there will be white light,
unnatural calm, a terrible thirst,

flowers to crush in her miniature fists,
days when the bike says 'hyacinth'
and then the chain comes off.

A long wait. No time to waste. Look—
he is pressing down on the pedals,
stretching the skin of the world.

Les Baillessats
for Emile

Sixteen panes in the cottage window—
one for each month of your life—
starting with bluest sky, top left,
reading across and down into the trees

where things get more complicated—
a stream that goes on and on about
where it's going and where it's been.
Pils the dog is sleeping on the driveway,

Mimi is tending her kittens somewhere
or perhaps they've been killed already,
seeing as their father is Mimi's brother Raaf,
a raven, gone wild, grass seeds in his fur,

who crept past me on the hillside at 6 a.m.
on his way to steal something from the house
as I sat among scrub oak and wild thyme
watching the sun colour Canigou.

*

There's so much to tell you. You see
everything, but won't remember it,
even though, each day, you remember the chickens
and take me by the hand and lead me there—

the rooster, with feathers of polished rust
and Lily, your favourite, shy and white.

Dogs, cats, chickens. Goats go past the gate
twice a day, led by Ursula, her cheeks

bright red from the weather. Thirty
or forty goats, with beards and fine horns,
bells whose clank carries over the slopes
when they're coming down for evening milking.

You stood at the gate while they filed past
one morning at eight—you were so excited
your arms pumped as if you were beating
the great big drum of life.

*

In the afternoon, while you sleep,
the goats come up into the trees
on the other side of the stream—
the buck with his long black beard

and devilish eyes—he's the model of a devil—
goes up on his hind legs to chomp
whole bunches of bright green leaves.
The Cathars who lived here believed all flesh

the devils' work, and that souls passed
from body to body until they received
the sacrament of Consolation—
what did they make of these butterflies—

the yellow-green, black-orange, orange, red—
drifting down, so many, all different,
as if somewhere in the wings, upstream,
a new soul hatched, each minute, with new wings.

*

Hard fields the Cathars worked
marked out with rows of stones:
they meant no harm. They're gone. Butterflies
and damselflies: somewhere in your body,

after all, you will remember this—
lizards so small and still and quick,
warm gritty stones they loved
losing their heat little by little

as the sun moves across a sky
of medieval blue, and the stream
babbles, meaninglessly,
after all: some things that concern us

don't concern us. One of the hens laid
a tiny egg, and Erin brought it to you—
miniature, perfect. Soon you will wake
in the present, which is full of consolation.

Mauve

Mauve, the blue,
from edge to edge

then all the river—
the river Mauve—

many millstreams,
many mills

grind the grain of days—
the old days, that come back

one by one, all summer,
dressed in mauve.

*

Mirrorshards—
the dragonfly

helps you reassemble
iridescent splinters into

something resembling
the same face, lined

with broken light—
a pool of sky, its waterskin

unhidden by
the dragonfly.

*

Acres of slate I walk
in my chalk boots, disproving

formula after formula.
Time swam

in my hands
for all I care—

slate's mauve tint,
mountains of cloud—

it will rain
and it will rain.

*

Mauve, a moment
leaves

move over
light

arrives,
divides,

leaving room
beside hard

white
time.

Poppy

Each seed wrote
a red correction

(history's bee needs
so much help)—

the sound of marching,
a note in the margin,

harvest after
harvest, until

the land
forgets.

*

Chicory
mirrors

an airmail
sky:

Mother,
all is

peace. The
war

goes
on.

The Present

I'd given my father a humble figure
carved from dark stone, smooth as if river-worn,
face drawn in with fine white lines;
fine white lines ran down its limbs.

It was a crystalline day in spring
or autumn; he was walking
down Salamanca Road where it turns
and runs above the rose garden—

a glint of harbour in the distance,
a spring in his step because he'd discovered
a whole new place to park—
a wide street lined with pōhutukawa

and angle spaces—all of them empty—
marked with clean white lines.
He was wearing his fine grey suit—
pink cheeks, grey suit—

and was heading
down into the city
as if he had business
to attend to.

My father was surprised—
not, as I would have expected
to receive a carved stone figure—
but that I thought it necessary

to give him a present at all—
it wasn't Christmas, it wasn't
his birthday, it was just
a fine clear day in spring or autumn

so I told him
it was because he'd had a rough year,
what with his having
died and everything.

In The Cemetery

The dead are not here,
sunbathing in their granite suits.

Or have become these birds:
the serin serenades itself,

the redstart stars
in its own black night of feathers,

stops on top of a sepulchre
to let its hymn cross

into gossip—this
crisp ripping of

these, our
deeds.

Robins

Robins hover
during the meeting
over the reddening vine.

I can no longer hear you
but sometimes I can see
what you were saying.

The Sunflower

for Stuart Francis Wilson Johnston, 1931–2004

One young bloom in a vase or jar, breath-
takingly yellow. And her
hands, in the morning light, the way
they arrange and rearrange. Death
brings lilies, but someone has sent a sunflower:
this is our penance, staring at the sun,
its blind eye, its ragged halo. The day,
in the end, took to its bed
before the day was over, taking thee
with it. Soon this flower, too, will be dead,
its summer of wondering done
about the sun, petal by petal: *loved me;*

didn't know how; did, unsayably so. It leaves me
as he left us, in the dark. From one breath
to the next, he'd deflect a question: in his the-
ology, *I, me, mine* were just not done.
But he was on speaking terms with death
so we can stare at the sunflower all day.
His heavenly father's garden was further
than we were prepared to go—its bed
of blood-red roses, its promises, its premises, the way
everything had been arranged; 'dead'
a manner of speaking, under the sun.
We counted ourselves lucky, hour by hour,

and by the minutes of the sunflower
(*he doesn't, he does, he doesn't know me*),
each in his or her own way worshipping the sun
and coming to other arrangements with death—

that it is the end, in the abstract. And then one day
someone calls, and you take a deep, deep breath.
Sister nor'wester, southerly brother—
into the mind of the man we guess our way,
blind and deaf, senseless, because he is dead.
From the end of the earth I will cry unto thee,
as daughters and sons have always done,
for words unsaid. The riverbed

was dry and I was thirsty. By your bed,
near the end, we could count our
blessings: each day,
for one thing, and though it was winter, the sun.
A sisterly sixth sense, when death
began to bloom, flew me
from the end of the earth. In a week you were dead
but we shouldered one another
through the brittle days before you went away.
You talked and talked, as you'd always done,
of all but you, till you were out of breath.
I would have liked to hear—despite your fear of the-

atre (so foolish was I, and ignorant, before thee)—
about your mother, for instance, who took to bed
when the going got tough; and the sun
that had burned a dead-
ly thirst into your father's breath;
but the hard facts I craved, my mother
knew, were the same stones, day

after day, that you buried in death-
ly silence, so that in this inscrutable way
you could build—for you, for her, for six including me—

a house, a plain, safe house, with a sunflower
in the garden. 'That which is done

is that which shall be done'
is all very well in the-
ory, but what if the sun
were black, and the book dead
wrong, and the interval under death
demanded a father
as unlike his father as day
and night? A breath
of wind reaches me
from the rose-bed;
in its vase or jar the sunflower
nods politely. Halfway

across the Channel, halfway
between waking and sleeping, my mind undone,
I had, as luck would have it, something of an inkling. The day
had been long; as I lay in the boat's narrow bed
a breaking wave of black joy lifted me and left in me
knowledge so dark it shone. I held my breath.
Fear fell away, of death, and other
fears; the end, in the end, was the darkest jewel. I was dead
tired, and fatigue's mysterious flower
spoke perhaps in tongues. But that black sun
still shines—a talisman, obsidian, a bright antithe-
sis. Its darkness made light of death

at most, however, for me; the death
of someone else is something else. Your way
led over the border; I am a stranger with thee,
and a sojourner, but wherever I am, my place in the sun
you prepared. His earthly power

spent, your god, to us, is dead,
but it was your belief that gave us breath,
the life we take for granted every day.
What sense of your sense will I take with me?
How much of your world will we hand on?
Just before the end, on the wall beside your bed,
Peter pinned Leonardo's St Anne. Her

smile—is it wry?—reminds me of you, and her
hand-on-hip benevolence. Wherever death
leads, we can meet here. The power
of light in van Eyck and Vermeer. The breath
of Wallace Stevens, overhearing his way
to work. Every Henry James you read in bed,
destiny and destiny like night and day.
The valedictory music of 'The Dead'.
Thou hast set our iniquities before thee
but when all—or almost all—is said and done
sometimes it seemed you believed no less than me
that we live in an old chaos of the sun.

That there is nothing new under the sun
but much of it is mystery: this my mother knows. Her
psychological eye revised your the-
ological line. They'd converge, anyway,
at the library—your rain-cloud, your seed-bed.
You read and read and read. And saved your breath
not to write yourself, but to make each day

bloom and turn. The astonishing flower,
head full of edible seeds, bows down dead:
this is the credible sense of its death,
that here, where its turning is done,
other journeys begin. It seems to me

you believed what you believed, but it strikes me,
too, that the seeds you sowed, in the mind's sun,
mattered most. (Sometimes they grew a bed
of nails: you were often 'sick to death'
of fools and fads and feuds, the way
they shut out the sun.) Flower
of wonder, flower of might: if I see thee
on the other side, when I am dead,
I'll know there is an other
side. Till then, while we have breath,
our burgeoning work is not done:
what we have been given is a rich, difficult day

that could go on without us, nevertheless, all day,
whistling a cryptic tune. It comes to me
in the conservatory, where we catch a little sun:
I didn't know you well, and then you went away
but in the day of my trouble I will call upon thee
because you were a man to get things done.
In its vase or jar, the young sunflower
I imagine has served its purpose. Beneath its bed,
all along, the river was flowing—deep, where death
knows more than we. Sylvia puts on her
gardening gloves to gather the dead
roses. Man cannot utter it, but under his breath:

'Remember me, my loves, when I am dead.'
Rest on memory's sea-bed: we will swim down to thee.
And in our own blue day, we will gaze at death
the way this one young bloom would gaze at the sun.
In the garden of the living, my mother stops for breath.
Thou thy worldly task hast done. And seeds rain from the
        sunflower.

Aitche

for Denis O'Connor

Thank you for aitche
—its itch, its ache—
thank you for shifting the posts

and lifting the ships
—Minerva, Clifton, Lancashire Witch—
their wakes, their lists of ghosts:

say Mayo, say Galway
or Dublin, say,
travelling from or travelling to,

the aitchless generations'
aching voices coming through,
their silent aspirations coming true.

Her Eyes

Irises green as the sea—
as if he could be rescued by danger—

pupil as in pupil, with
much to teach—

a pale lake, opaquely opal—
Ah! semiprecious one,

he thought (it wasn't true)—
this one, she sees through me—

she's the one who'll
see me through.

Great Aunt

Home star, broken wheel,
bride not spoken for,

where stars abound
she is among them,

where the great aren't
coming home

she will wait
the sun around,

she will stand
her ground.

So

From far above, the aerials
looked like Chinese characters. So,

sighed the scholar: so many to learn.
And so many TV channels—

the cooking shows, the non-stop news,
an action film with a thoughtful scene:

a car winds up a hill and one of the characters
sees the aerials. So, he says. So

you see, after all, he was
something of a scholar.

If Mauve

If mauve, a life
brightens—sound-

less, a deer, in
the invisible

forest—of beams,
a great frame,

beneath the stone
that gives,

a little,
for you.

FROM

Fits and Starts

2016

The Otorhinolaryngologist

After having asked me to say Ah
after having himself said Ah

the otorhinolaryngologist
guided me silently over the ancient carpet

to a small white room with two low stools
and handed me a bulb on the end of a cord:

this, he said, is a cold light,
and I want you to put it in your mouth.

He flicked a switch and we sat in the dark
lit only by my ghostly face.

*

Suddenly I understood
history, weather, time,

I could see the skeleton
of every memory

the how of war
the knife of every scar;

everything I'd never learned
burned brightly in my mind—

calculus, zoology,
epistemology—

*

I could see the otorhinolaryngologist
seeing me, I could see

how good he was, and beyond him
where evil came from,

the origins of language, and languages,
the splintering chaos

of thought, slowed down
till I could hear its ticking,

the birth of galaxies, planets and stars,
sped up so I could grasp all in an instant

*

but once his eyes had adjusted
to the dark in which my sinuses glowed

the otorhinolaryngologist
extinguished the light in my head

and turned on the light
in the small white room

plunging me back into
familiar mists

through which I swam to
pay him and to leave—

*

a cold wind blew down the street,
I was hungry, and stumbled,

hankering, perplexed,
abandoned again

to hunting for something
in the hollow spaces

in the voiceless spaces
filled with the sound of footsteps

hurrying
into the dark.

So Dad

So Dad (no more
sad songs) happy

to have reached the very idea
after so much arriving:

permanent yesterday. Now
that you're a xylophone,

monsieur, life is soft,
but there are moments of striving

to hear, above the sodden ground,
the sound of padded hammers.

Agnes

I have one Moonlight
who married into my tree—

Agnes Moonlight, born
St Vigeans, Angus,

eighteen thirty-six,
September three.

I have been unable to locate
a death date

for her. Does this
help? Do you

have Agnes Moonlight
in your tree?

Afghanistan

Do you remember the music?
Do you remember the trees?

I remember this,
said the river:

The snow will melt,
the poppies will grow,

the opium will be harvested.
The foreigners will come,

the foreigners will go.
It will begin to snow.

*

Headless in a bloody pool, his master:
Ahmad Shah, at 24, fled east

to Kandahar, the gathered clan,
rival upon rival, till a rival laid

a strand of wheat across his head.
Blades of grass between their teeth,

yokes of cloth around their necks—
to show they would be his cattle—

chiefs who have always shared power
by choosing the weakest as leader.

*

'Grief clings to my heart like a snake.
I forget the throne of Delhi

when I remember
the mountaintops of my Afghan land.'

Because of his fondness for pearls,
Abdali became Durrani,

who looted a caravan of treasure,
paid an army to sack west and east—

from Khorasan to India,
the emperor of grief.

*

I would not pray,
so my father put me out;

I went to Kabul
but it was still Afghanistan:

a few hours of power a day,
constant extortion.

Two million, three: why are we here?
War killed as many. This much is clear:

blood on the road to Kandahar,
bones on the road to Panjshir.

*

Here's Miss Snowflake in Peshawar
with Congressman Wilson—

Good Time Charlie—packing
CIA money for Stingers

that know how to find the heat
at the heart, from here to Herat,

of what he would call the Cold War—
'It was very clandestine,' recalled Miss Snowflake.

'It was just very, very exciting to be in that room
with those men with their huge white teeth.'

*

Agfa, or Fuji, washed out
seventies photographs with flares:

Daoud could be said
in Agfacolor or Afghacolor to have been,

to have been seen,
in the shadow of the mountains,

in the light of later fates,
as the least of the worst

before the shutter cut us
back to darkness:

*

The Aryan night,
the Achaemenid night,
the Persian night,
the Bactrian night,
the Seleucid night,
the Mauryan night,
the Scythian night,
the Parthian night,
the Kushan night,
the Sassanid night,
the Kidarite night,
the Hephthalite night,
the Samanid night,
the Ghaznavid night,
the Seljukid night,
the Ghorid night,
the Mongol night,
the Timurid night,
the Mughal night,
the Durrani night,
the Victorian night,
the Edwardian night,
the Barakzai night,
the Soviet night,
the Mujahed night,
the Taliban night

and now because you are sending more men
you want us to say the sun has risen.

*

I would not pray, it would
only make things more Afghan, you

understand? If
you don't understand, there are

Afghans in the park (there
are questions in the dark)—

Hazara, Aimak, Pashtun, Uzbek, Tajik:
there are Afghans becoming Afghans

in the dark, in the park,
why don't you ask them.

*

Someone will come for the turban and shoes.
Someone will come for Afghanistan

and find Afghanistan:
gate blown through a gate,

shards that have been shards for years,
shards that were only yesterday.

Hazara, Aimak, Pashtun, Uzbek, Tajik:
someone will come as they have always come

over the mountains, over and over,
from Afghanistan to Afghanistan.

Hunch

I was in love with your shrink
in my dream, she said

tell me your dream, so I
told her my waking—

page black with ink
I would have to unwrite—

little by little I saw the light
turn into a blizzard. My head

filled with rain.
I hunched my way down the mountain.

Woodwind

for Rostropovich

A red ribbon
in the region of the second clarinet

a forest of people a sudden clearing
a flashback
a backlash—

replaces the mouthpiece, the reed,
is ready for the cellist—

a body between rivers
in the region of the reeds

another, and another

distant cloud with a beard of rain

oil and reeds
smoke
Babylonian dust

but no running water
and the living, silent

the big man blew
through this man
and this man

looking for a pure note—

a ribbon of red
a marvellous acoustic—
an otherwise empty hall—

the second clarinet
pulls a ribbon through—

a rustle, as of reeds
giving in

to the slightest wind.

Half-Life

A kind of dark green time
fills the canal and flows

slowly so as not to wake the baby
into the neighbourhood of health we push

across the currents of worry—
power, rumour and data—

particles parting and falling apart,
beautiful path of everything halving

or just the road to school, and a bird
rehearsing: What have we learned?

*

Research and development will get you
halfway, then start to decay

exponentially. This is my alibi—I
was not quite there,

where they do things indifferently
to prove their love.

Stare through their objective:
it brings things closer to thee.

X billion people. A dollar a day.
Drink Lucky Number Tea.

*

'Compassion fatigue,' 'comfort zone,'
'the problem of other minds'—

every day the waiter brings us
whichever soup he chooses

of nature and nurture,
of fog. The facts themselves

lack taste,
leaving the trees in clouds,

leaving us in autumn, autonomous,
under the chemical weather.

*

Alea. Les ailes. What ails?
You could use an alias—

yellow ballerina,
shepherdess of the streams.

She's waiting for the downtown
evolution bus, she's

drinking Lucky Number Tea,
she's waiting for us

to name the bird of change
and change its name.

*

Molecules break down for you, reliably unstable.
Breakfast is served at the periodic table.

Doom was a mood
marooned in canal-time, horse-

nonsense under the chestnuts
whose branches seemed willing to help.

The moon's a bad candle.
It's not about you.

When you come back, think to bring
a loaf of rough warm bread.

Leviticus

Echo sought a tree to stand under,
someone to explain—

how shalt thou love
as thyself? She tried

to imagine having that
tank of gas, roaming—

no scapegoat—
all over the landscape.

The spirit of the law was all she had.
If she could only love her echo better.

Deuteronomy

South of the past,
dreaming she was still alive,

Echo came in low, under the dateline,
over the mudflats, mirroring.

To see the plane kiss its shadow
she would have to be somewhere else

but she sees it, she sees everything
kissing everything. She was the pool,

his face bending lovely, lips
touching down.

Joshua

Mourn in vain for
gone trees.

Knowing such love
destructive,

Echo ran her hands
over their last stands,

picked away thick hammered flakes
to stroke the inner bark—

forgetfully smooth.
Grief does not soothe.

Judges

Hunger renders her
almost invisible

then disappears itself.
Was it possible not to think

and become that thought,
to walk right out of your life?

She gave her word. She kept her word.
I wanted me to sound like me.

Sometimes the wind carries her voice,
sometimes she has to carry it herself.

Ruth

Whither thou goest, a falling feeling
becomes familiar, the selfsame song

is sirens, party laughter. I rue not
the day but it is foreign—

my sad heart goes out and comes home
late, its memory is full.

I own that I see because I look, but
what else is there to glean in this city?

Because thy people shall be my people
I'm as sick for here as I'm sick for home.

I Samuel

Imagine an active satellite, Echo,
listening to the words of the prophets

over the land of the broken promise,
dreaming gone trees because their missingness

goes deep. The king of my heart is hunting
the king of my mind: I hear their shadows,

the satellite passing. Echo,
bring the things omitted—

codes, a spade—to place
between these lines.

II Samuel

Photograph she'd seen somewhere: a tree
unearthed by workmen, where she'd grown,

and how with a rippling she saw
the whole forest rise and fall.

She tiptoed out of there, she ran
from explanation to explanation—

will we survive without these trees?
Satellite evidence. Smoke thereof.

How we were felling and clearing
a graveyard for our children.

I Kings

Breath was a thread that led back
to where Echo rose and was praised

as if praise could banish dismay.
That she had a blue tank of. It dragged:

she didn't lack lack. It did hunt
in all seasons. Cursed to the limit

to mimic, she prays: for whirlwinds,
for landslides, for fire, and after

the fire a still small voice: her
breath. She tends its echo.

II Kings

Neither the soul of a tree nor a dryad:
Echo wanted to be the tree,

to survive by sealing off
anything stricken. Instead she felt

in her bones the strain
of orbital decay. Of dismay.

Daughter of a voice, she recalls
a team with too many members

and when they drew the line
it went right through her mind.

I Chronicles

My father invented the cloud. It grew
out of his brow. He was always thinking.

Doubt? Data? He thought of water,
poured from glass to glass.

You will notice I use the passive voice,
which implies an invisible hand.

A steady hand steadily pouring.
And when one glass is full

and one glass empty, the hand
will take the empty glass and smash it.

Ezra

Forests couldn't contain her rage.
Echo chose a grove of oaks,

listened to their rustling,
hoping the gods would tell her

what to do with her anger.
If she hacked rocks and stacked them up,

she would only want to tear them down.
As when the temple foundation was laid

with trumpets, cymbals, a shout of joy
so loud no one heard the old men weeping.

Nehemiah

Though you rebuild the sheep gate,
the tower of Meah, the fish gate—

though you repair the broad wall,
the dung gate, the gate of the fountain,

the wall of the pool of Siloah—
though you earnestly rebuild

the going up to the armoury
at the turning of the wall—

though you sanctify the gates—
though you build a wall.

Esther

When did memory begin? She
threw a rock into that black

hoping to strike up a conversation.
Who were you to give me life?

She recalled the hangings—*white, green and blue,*
fastened with cords of linen and purple—

and the hangings of Haman and his sons:
how could a word be so treacherous?

A slip of the tongue. A lapse.
A million kinds of black.

Job

Where the forest comes down to the sea
I should have been as though I had not been.

I'm the hermit crab, hauling
this hell of a thought from hole to hole.

Starfish, anemone, barnacle, shrimp
gone from the memory pool—

everything is evidence that we have
entered into the treasures of the snow.

And I haul my shell of a name
as if I'm to blame.

Psalms

Bones of smoke, of ash, of air—
I may tell all my bones, said Echo, but

I am the fool who hath said in his heart
I will make a fitful tune

by bonelight, if
you will play along.

At Bec-Hellouin the monks, half-awake,
are hard at work. One arrives late,

dragging his habit over his head,
having already begun the song.

Ecclesiastes

Echo and the Preacher
dance. Their bodies

whirleth about continually.
Don't be in such a rush,

he mumbles in her ear.
How can she tell him

that she can't dance
with the sound of her own voice?

She fell in love with the river. The river
was falling in love with the sea.

Isaiah

Why did you choose this particular myth?
Because it made the same noise as my myth.

Can you describe the sound it produced?
It resembled the memory of a memory.

And the original recollection, what was that of?
A rustling before memory began.

Where does all the stuff about trees come from?
Each absent tree cast two shadows.

Can you recommend a good book?
Can you recommend a good life?

Jeremiah

Echo's thought-boat rode
the overlapping line

of thriving and dying, its peaks of hope,
its valleys rich with failure. She wanted

to rescue the kingdom from itself,
to light its lamp and polish its wings. She

needed a little less news, a moment
of nothing, of nowhere. There was

so much meaning in her life.
She didn't know what any of it meant.

Ezekiel

Echo stepped
and stepped away from fate.

The wind whistles and won't listen.
She wants to flesh out this frame,

to test the myth for mystery.
If you can live with missingness

it X-rays the days,
it cuts away.

These bones shall live.
They shine with disbelief.

Alpha

Beware of wolf logic
as you would be wary of

bumping your head in the mountains,
reaching for something to say—

wolf-teeth in your shoulder
wanting you to howl:

make yourself a mountain—
full of weather, but

a mountain,
even so.

Bravo

Every gesture offers
this possibility

but there will be no applause
for even the most beautiful of your thoughts—

in which you wash ashore, beyond thought,
and set off into the hinterland

of laughter and
suffering. So

in advance, over and over,
forever let me say bravo.

Charlie

Whatever you do don't
do that—

Charlie hurts, and Charlie,
the mention of his name—

he got sent off
to hospital—

if you see Charlie
but you won't see Charlie—

he was brown,
I broke him down.

Delta

I flew Delta
from Boston to Austin,

Chicago Pittsburgh New York.
I had an epiphany in New York—

the world wasn't so bad or hard—
then I met your mother.

As for the third point of the triangle,
out where the river meets the sea—

the one that helps you to get your bearings—
strictly speaking I won't be there.

Echo

Echo in her cave of air played with radio—
e e e e—

borneo stereo clifftop whisper—
love me love you stop don't stop—

just as she seized each sound she'd feel
its roots ripped out of her head.

She knows what she is missing:
only the dead have souls.

She prays for sleep. She is incomplete.
She has been found wanting.

Foxtrot

The French think he's American,
the Americans, English.

The English, Irish, Scots and Welsh
say he sounds Australian.

Only the Australians
can tell where he's from—

because he says dance
as in aunts, not ants—

not that he can dance, he can't,
not even with his aunt.

Golf

Before you know it
you're back where you started—

by the racecourse, by the camping ground,
where the small polluted stream

misremembers its name. You're out there
with your family tree,

your sandwiches,
the receipt for your fee,

and then before you know it
you're back where you started.

Hotel

When Echo shut the door and sat on the floor
that was a hotel, she guessed—

somewhere to stay when she found herself
a country made foreign by longing.

A host of voices overhead. She blurred. How
was she feeling? Alone in a field. She was the field,

too. She didn't have to think about it.
Something flocked there—returning birds.

If she could rock her baby self to sleep.
If they would let her cross the border then.

India

If they would let her cross the border then
Echo would have to prepare herself for

the Fourteen Unanswerable Questions—
concerning eternity, infinity and death,

both, neither, and, or—to which the Buddha replied
'Did you pack your bags yourself?' and

'Have you any previous convictions?'
On the plane she looked at *The Last Pictures*

and there was the Union Carbide ad—
'Bringing science to India.'

Juliet

That's the boy, she'll say,
that's the boy in you—

sitting on some bench, or beach,
gazing into the same

maddening distance. It's
the boy in her, she says,

that likes the girl in you. Ah, to be
a person, that's hard

enough. Sleep now. Get some sleep,
that's the boy.

Kilo

Ten years of pointing at
fruit in the market, I think I've

mastered the language.
Ah, to be an artist—

once you've mastered mastery
the rest is child's play—

mystery, truth,
the beautiful fruit

and the local people, smiling, look—
you've won them over, too.

Lima

Comes a day—hey hey—you know you'll never go
some places in your life and one is Lima.

There was a map of the world on the wall
at home and the game was to name a place—

one of us lost and the other was lost
in shades of blue, in terrain, in the legend—

lines for trains, for planes, for liners,
directions you'd have to follow

never knowing if they'd lead you
towards or away from Lima.

Mike

All I remember
is your password, all

I remember is
your America—

bourbon, burritos,
ranch dressing—your joke

is all I remember—'great
haircut, wrong planet'—

all I remember is
'miss you already'.

November

Fresh dreams for breakfast,
fresh mistakes for lunch.

Three o'clock eats two o'clock.
Four crows eat a parakeet.

My face is glad.
My blood is sad.

The river of wisdom rushes past,
head down—it has

somewhere to get to and no,
today it will not donate.

Oscar

Why it is dark inside the brain.
Why there are things I can't explain.

What the wind said
when it finally stopped talking.

Where we all came from.
Why you can't get there by walking.

How there are people who put down roots.
Why I wouldn't go that far.

How I married distance
and how close we are.

Papa

By which I mean not the soft rock
upstream from where my father was born—

bluish, hardly rock at all, more like a cloudy day—
nor the yaw and pitch of his father's ship,

his father's jig, his father's reel—
nor your father reaching for the dial

in the seventies, as if to turn down
an offer from God—to be softly rocked—

but the word itself, when you call,
that falls and continues to fall.

Quebec

Having pursued your train as far as Quebec,
having just ashes amid which to hunt and peck,

having tried to cash your rubber cheque,
having your swansong around my neck,

having abandoned your call and beck,
I banked instead bitter disaffec-

tion, I contemplated the travel sec-
tion, I set out in praise of a fresh direc-

tion. You'll find the rest of the trek
in the whole qasida, of which this is just the wreck.

Romeo

If it rains, call me—
from the cradle of prehistory,

from a cave, if it rains.
Don't call me, it'd kill me—

it's raining, call me,
I'm dying anyway,

of prehistory, the cradle, a cave,
of the fact that I cracked

like a nut when
you looked my way.

Sierra

I was angry with my brother—
couldn't he see? I had so many bags

to carry across the hills.
There was nothing he could do.

He tried to give me money.
He was not my brother.

Then my anger left me, it was just
something else to carry

up the steep ridge that fell away steeply
on both sides of the family.

Tango

When I was in the trough
being eaten by the pig Life,

I looked up at the stars—
I thought I saw your sign and my sign

doing the tango.
We lit up the night.

We rearranged the universe.
Everything was going to be all right.

I'm trying to get my head around it
when the pig's twinkling eyes come down again.

Uniform

Only at fifteen, Vladimir,
were clouds allowed to wear trousers.

Southerlies drove the gulls up the valley
to shit in flocks on fields

where clouds would ruck and roam
and want to go home.

Once I was kneed in the gut and chucked
all over the coach's suit.

By then it was raining. A suit, Vladimir,
because the past will be formal.

Victor

Convolvulus, thought Echo, or maybe poison ivy—
vee for vegetation, two for weedy species—

convolvulus, or even us . . .
Down on her knees in the weeds is she weeding

or filling their little ear-trumpets with names—
my moonflower, my morning glory . . .

most of my thoughts are weeds, she thought.
The sound as she weeds is the sound of her putting

something or someone
out of her mind.

Whiskey

Sensei, they call him—Master,
on account of his technical perfection

but dealing with Sensei is kabuki
under water. Will you inherit my weakness

for not going there, for
watching the movie instead—

its Sensei, its ramen, its kabuki whiskey?
Some people have kabuki in the blood—

let them make the trip, and send back paper birds,
each explaining one of Sensei's words.

X-ray

Here's a picture of my life—no heart of gold,
silver tongue or will of iron,

just the bones of the story
surrounded by clouds.

I would have disappeared
but my bones spoke up—

like Mrs Roentgen's—
I have seen my death,

she said, and
went on living.

Yankee

It was on the bungee jump
I was introduced to

the art of oscillation.
I left myself in the lurch

from yackety-yack to yada yada
from roughly something to strictly nada—

having tasted weightlessness,
the world on a string, upside-down—

it was on the bungee jump
my smile became a frown.

Zulu

Youyou says Echo in Morocco—
ululation is what she needs,

its fuzzy logic, its vacillation.
She would hear herself uttered

at the limit
and beyond. Let's

widen the page and zigzag hard
into the margin—

there she stands,
among the people of heaven.

Acknowledgements

Heartfelt thanks to all those who have provided encouragement, advice and support over the years, especially Jenny Bornholdt, Greg O'Brien, Fergus Barrowman, Bill Manhire, Sarah Maxey, Peter Black, Mary Macpherson, Christine Lorre, Denis O'Connor, Clare Dunleavy, John Moriarty, Stephen James, Emma Neale, Nadine and Thierry Ribault, and Jim Siegel. Special thanks to C.R., V.H., H.N. and L.B.

Grateful thanks to the editors of publications where some of these poems first appeared: *100 Words* (USA), *Booknotes, The Bulletin, First XV, Fulcrum, Landfall, London Magazine, London Review of Books, Meanjin, Metro, North & South, NZ Listener, Poetry* (Chicago), *Poetry Review, Poetry Wales, The Poet's Voice* (Austria), *Printout, Quote Unquote, Scripsi, Snorkel, Sport, Tabla, Times Literary Supplement, Trout, Turbine* and *Verse* (UK).

The author gratefully acknowledges the assistance of Creative New Zealand and its predecessor the Queen Elizabeth II Arts Council for the award of the 1991 Louis Johnson New Writer's Bursary (to write *How to Talk*), an Established Writer's Bursary (to write *The Sounds*), and two project grants (to write *Birds of Europe* and *Sol*).

Many thanks to the University of Iowa and Creative New Zealand for a residency at the 1995 International Writing Program at the University of Iowa, where many of the poems in *The Sounds* were written. Thanks also to the Conseil départemental du Nord, France, for a residency in 2005 at the Villa Marguerite Yourcenar, where many of the poems in *Sol* were completed.

The first part of 'Roundabout' is comprised of quotations from John Ashbery, Robert Browning, William Cowper,

Paul Muldoon and James Joyce.

'Afghanistan' contains a quotation from *My Enemy's Enemy*, by George Crile III (Atlantic Books, 2003), and adapts a line from a poem by Rumi.

'Agnes' is a found poem from a public message board on ancestry.com.

The sequence 'Echo in Limbo' contains quotations from the King James Bible; Ovid's *Metamorphoses*, translated by A. D. Melville (Oxford University Press, 1986); and Martin Buber, *I and Thou*, translated by Walter Kaufmann (Charles Scribner's Sons, 1970).

The sequence 'Do You Read Me?' was first published in 2013 in a not-for-sale edition of fifty copies with photographs and illustrations by Sarah Maxey. A second edition was published in 2014 by Long Face Press.

How to Talk was dedicated to my parents, Stuart and Sylvia Johnston. *The Sounds* and *Birds of Europe* were dedicated to Christine Lorre. *Sol* was dedicated to Emile Johnston and the memory of Stuart Johnston (1931–2004). *Fits & Starts* was dedicated to Emile, Oscar and Louise Johnston.

Index of titles

Index of first lines